My name is

_____

and I love my twelve Imams!

Sun Behind
The Cloud

1. Imam Ali (as)

On the night of hijra, Prophet Muhammad escaped from Makkah to go towards Medina. Some people wanted to attack the Prophet that night. He asked Imam Ali to sleep in his bed. Imam Ali was so brave and slept there even though it was dangerous. He said it was the best night's sleep he'd had!

How will you try to be brave?

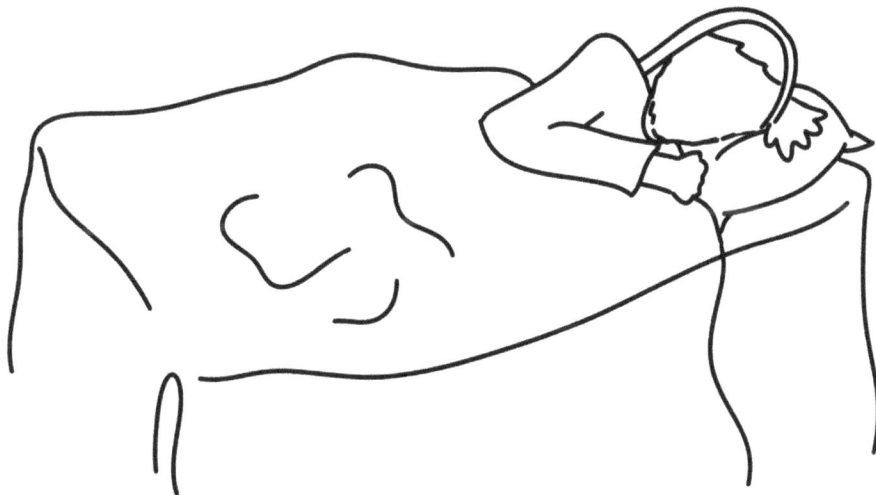

2. Imam Hasan (as)

Prophet Muhammad loved Imam Hasan so much! He would carry him on his shoulders and say "Hasan is from me, and I am from him. Allah loves the one who loves him. Hasan and Husayn are the two most special grand-children!"

How can you show the Ahlulbayt that you love them?

3. Imam Husayn (as)

The enemies of Islam thought that they had won when they killed Imam Husayn on the Day of Ashura in Karbala. Now millions of his followers call his name and visit him every year!

How can you keep the message of Imam Husayn alive?

4. Imam Sajjad (as)

Imam Sajjad loved to talk to Allah! He is called "Sajjad" because of how much he bowed down in prayer. Lots of his duas have been collected together in a book called Sahifa as-Sajjadiya.

Allah has said that He will answer the call of anyone who calls Him. What would you like to say to Allah?

5. Imam Baqir (as)

Imam Baqir was so clever! He showed people the difference between truth and falsehood so clearly and he was called "the one who cleaves knowledge open."

How can you try to gain knowledge?

6. Imam Sadiq (as)

Imam Sadiq taught thousands of students all about Allah, the world and even space! He was known for always telling the truth. As-Sadiq means "The Truthful One."

How can you try to always tell the truth?

7. Imam Kadhim (as)

One day, a servant of Imam Kadhim dropped what he was carrying on him by accident. The servant was scared but Imam Kadhim was not angry, he told his servant not to worry and then he freed him. Imam Kadhim was always calm and kind.

How can you calm down when you are angry?

8. Imam Ridha (as)

When it was time to eat, and the table had been laid, Imam Ridha would make sure all the servants sat down to eat too. Then he would sit with the servants and share his food.

How can you try to share your things?

9. Imam Jawad (as)

Imam Taqi al-Jawad was so generous! Every night, when most people were asleep, Imam Jawad would carry sacks of food and deliver them to the homes of all the needy people.

How can you help the needy?

10. Imam Hadi

Imam Hadi al-Naqi was placed under house arrest. Soldiers would guard his house and make sure he could not leave freely. When the soldiers watched the good behaviour and akhlaq of Imam Hadi, they began to love him and believe in him as an Imam.

What does your behaviour say about you?

11. Imam Askari (as)

Imam Askari had to keep the birth of his son a secret because his life was in danger. He would only show the new baby to his trusted companions who spread the news that the Mahdi was born! Imam Askari was careful to protect the Imam and spread goodness to everyone.

How can you spread goodness?

12. Imam Mahdi (as)

When Imam Mahdi returns, he will fill the world with love, hope and justice. That means that everything will be fair and no one will be oppressed. We are really looking forward to his return and we pray that he comes back quickly!

How can you prepare for his return?

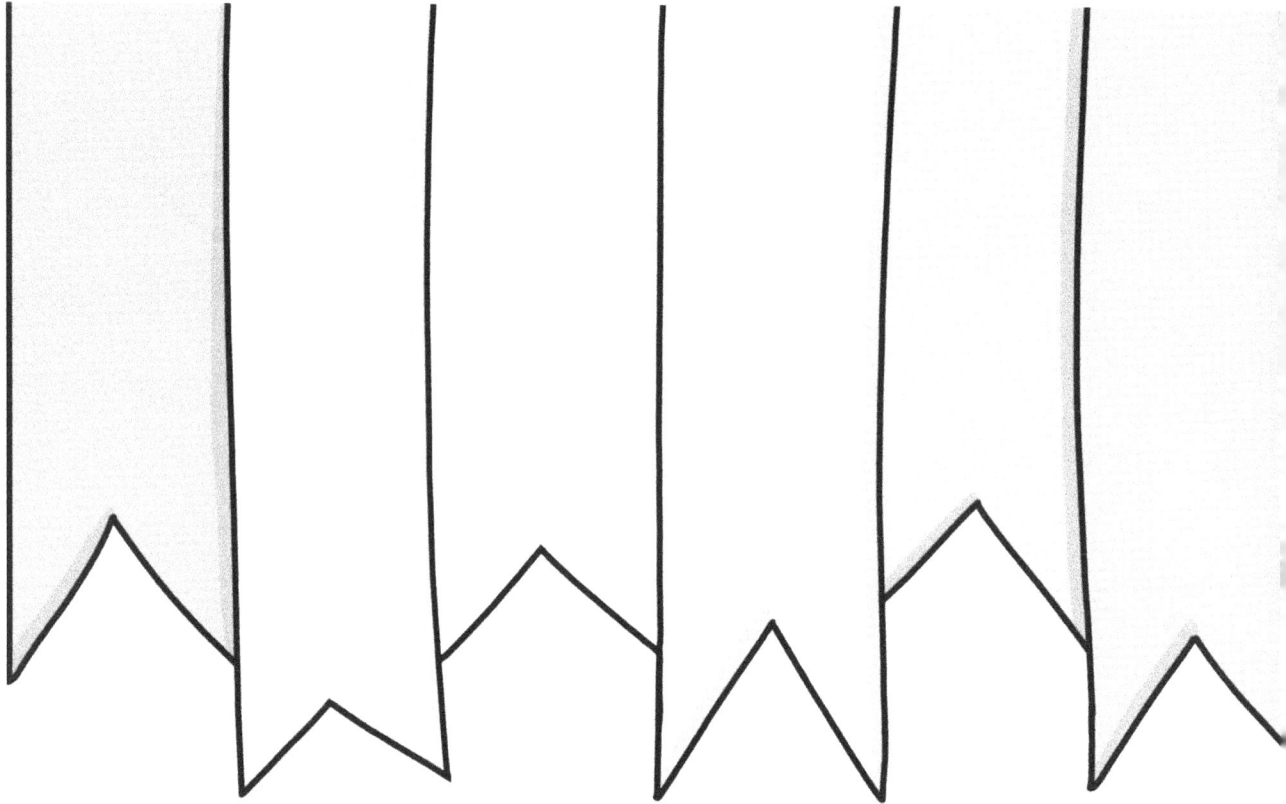

Can you remember the names of all the twelve
Imams? Try to write them out in order.

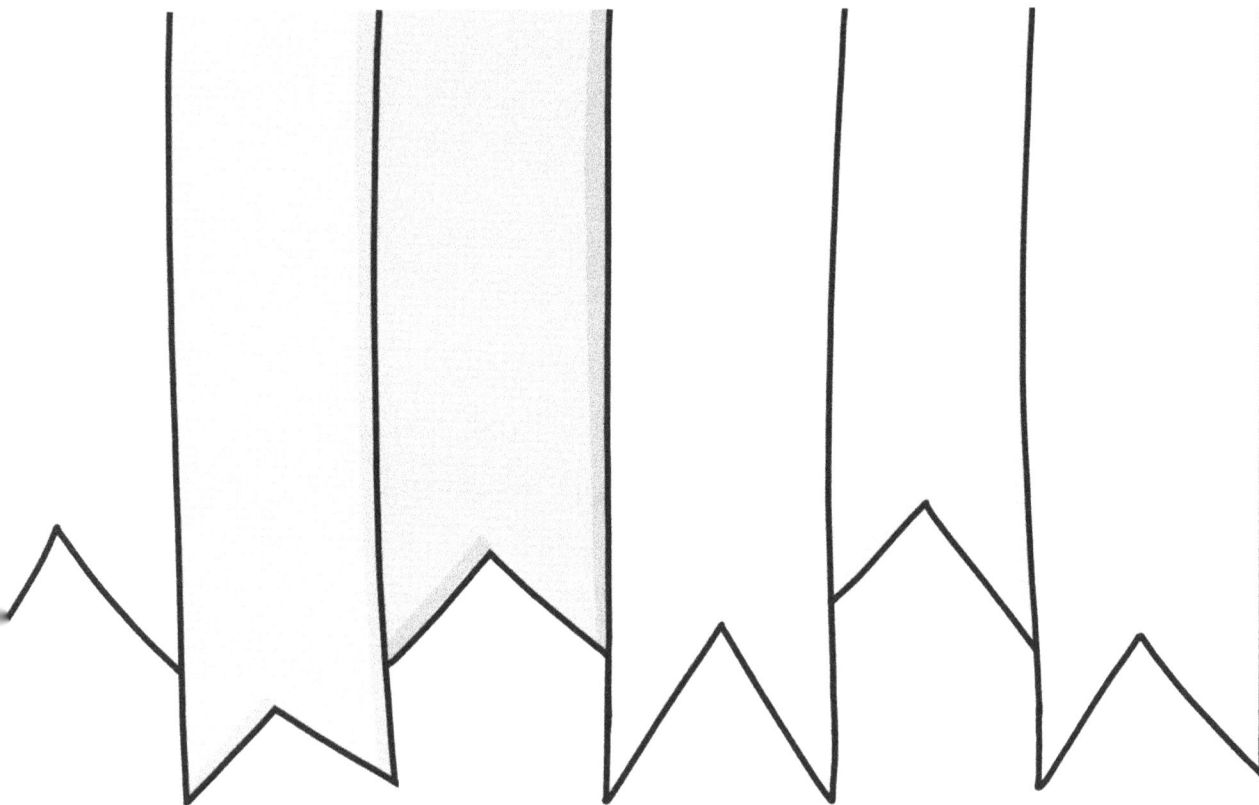

Send your salaams to the Ahlulbayt! Did you know that the reply to a salaam is wajib?

Assalamu Alyka Ya Imam!

Scan here to listen to the nasheed!
These are my Twelve Imams recited by Mulla Ali Fadhil

Published by Sun Behind The Cloud Publications

PO Box 15889 Birmingham, B16 6NZ

Illustrations by Hood n Cape

A CIP catalogue record of this book is available from the British Library
ISBN (Print): 978-1-908110-75-6

www.sunbehindthecloud.com

Sun Behind
The Cloud

www.ingramcontent.com/pod-product-compliance
Ingram Content Group UK Ltd.
Pitfield, Milton Keynes, MK11 3LW, UK
UKHW031936040325
4855UKWH00013B/452

9 781908 110756